**Date Due**

BRODART, CO.    Cat. No. 23-233-003    Printed in U.S.A.

ALSO BY BARBARA GUEST:

*The Location of Things*, Doubleday, 1960
*Poems*, Doubleday, 1962
*The Blue Stairs*, Corinth, 1968
*Moscow Mansions*, Viking, 1973
*Seeking Air* (a novel), Black Sparrow, 1977
*Biography*, Burning Deck, 1980
*Herself Defined: The Poet H. D. and Her World*, Doubleday, 1968
*Musicality*, Kelsey St. Press, 1988
*Fair Realism*, Sun & Moon, 1990

# thE COUNtESS fROM MiNNEAPOliS

© 1976 by Barbara Guest

Second edition, 1991, offset from the original letterpress edition.

*Some of the poems were first printed in ZZZZZ.*

*The cover by Keith Waldrop uses Robert Koehler's painting* Rainy Evening on Hennepin Avenue *by courtesy of the Minneapolis Institute of Arts.*

ISBN 0-930900-06-5 (pbk.) $8

*BARBARA GUEST*

# THE COUNTESS FROM ~ MINNEAPOLIS

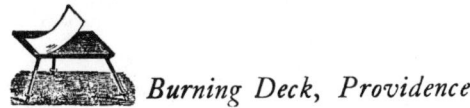
*Burning Deck, Providence*

# I

water wheels river turns river asides over and under falls splice rapid brown slow turn fist thrust signal ahead winter autumn water barge season thrice water bank bridge system barge deep search over falls rush edge search nearly there river bottoms watersurge bridgespread

# 2

Believe you Madam yon building of ice was built for thy pleasure?

I do.

Yu're right.

## 50 FLOORS

The glass stops midway skyways.
We look up.
The Indians look up.
My hood's up.
Their hood's down.
The glass gets stuck in my blue eye.
The glass rattles past their black eyes.
Crystal Court. King Flour's crystal court.
Blue eyes. Black eyes.
Gracefully King Flour floats down
on his quilt of white.
This quilt distributes free sifted flour over our
shoulders and when he lands near us he sticks
out his foot. I kiss it.
(The Indians spit on his toes.)

## THINKING OF YOU PROKOFIEF

The steam settled into the atmosphere
    steam in atmosphere
it was cold; so the steam did not move
    it became lonely as a field of daffodils
on the earth we kept looking up
on the horizon there was admiration
    those waltzes.

And the ivory of our lids felt vaporous
as if crevices were gained in the shell
where our eyes kept their hoods

    Thinking of you Prokofief
that tricky snow outside makes a steam indoors
and the china tea we brew keeps us quick
    as Prokofief
whose doors slam.

    Steam never lessens its latitude
in the sky
    like Prokofief
while many cars creep over the bridge sweating
finally equipped
    with their Mahler treads.

## RIVER ROAD STUDIO

Separations begin with placement
that black organizes the ochre
      both earth colors,

Quietly the blanket assumes its shapes
as the grey day loops along leaving
an edge (turned like leaves into something else),

Absolutes simmer as primary colors
and everyone gropes toward black
where it is believed the strength lingers.

I make a sketch from your window
the rain so prominent earlier
now hesitates and retreats,

We find bicycles natural
under this sky composed of notes,

Then ribbons, they make noises
rushing up and down the depots
at the blur exchanging
its web for a highway.

Quartets the quartets
are really bricks and we are
careful to replace them
until they are truly quartets.

## PORTRAIT OF MARY ROOD

After we left the building
We avoided the wire fencing
Being dressed in suede,
Like Spring more pliable than fur,
As a jar of oil allows the vinegar
To settle and the beans to quiver there
In new dressings of garlic and things.

Now in the garden with a black dog
Who shouts, "the snow's gone!" we
Celebrate weather and profiles and
The reliability of telephones that bring
Us together in the days of brightly lit
Stones, something like olives, or
As I said, beans, or as I say each
Time the door closes, Mary.
The Mary of R's and Crosses
Named for gestures with rains.

# 7

## EATING LAKE SUPERIOR CISCO SMOKED FISH

When the flageolets verts are finally cooked I shall be high on Mississippi rock water. The water flows over the rock leaving rich traces, unlike Alpine water that is so pure and sprightly like Fauntleroy Alpine deer, never touching rock or pebble. Pure. Yet feeble. Weak because the minerals are lacking. They only follow the tough arm of water that likes to mingle with the crowd and pick up its bitters in a dirty old smokey fist. Like Dickens.

# 8

## MUSINGS ON THE MISSISSIPPI

Although Paris has only one river, the Seine, this river behaves perfectly reasonably within the city limits, or arrondissements, approaching the isles with a courtliness and depositing its burdens with a verve one used to associate with the beret. A manner thus is maintained by the Seine which we define as raison d'être or Steak Diane or the French way of looking at things, sometimes it is true through a pigeonhole. Let's say neither New Yorkers or Parisians are inclined to "river worship." Certainly they are appreciative of the uses commercial and aesthetic of a river, yet neither is inclined to "go overboard" on the subject. Nothing at all here Oriental or Indian in that respect, or Hungarian either.

When I come to the subject of Minneapolis and its posture on the Mississippi, a confusion like a drought descends upon me. Minneapolis persistently nagged by the unreasonable river that both gladdens and disturbs her heart. I may become convinced that the only way to survive a long, unsettling, barren Minnesota winter is to sit in a hut by the log fire and looking past the tears of confusion and loneliness falling down my pinched and overheated cheeks study, chew, harry a map of Minneapolis. Thus one might survive until spring.

The following winter I would exact from my tree chopping, whiskey thawing, sullen recounting of woes active and mystical, the labor of studying the Mississippi River. Her windings, divagations, idiosyncracies, bridges, dredgings, falls, destructions which yearly drive a mortal to the furthest limits of that angst called despair triumphed over by a northern people only through the spiritual suicide of its artists.

## 9

## LEGENDS

Little Withergield was talking to his pal, Freotheric, as they walked in the woods near the Minnehaha Falls.

"I don't like skeletons, do you Freddy?"

"Nope. They scare me."

"It's the way their backs curve and sort of turn up into their skulls," said Withergield.

"When did you ever see a skeleton?" asked Freotheric.

"Last night."

"Where?"

"Here."

"That was no skeleton, silly. It was Hiawatha."

"Hiawatha's no skeleton."

"How do you know?"

"I seen him a lot. He's real strong. Strong enough to hold Minnehaha in his arms."

"That ain't Minnehaha."

"Who is it then, smarty?"

"A skeleton."

Just then a boulder went crashing over the Falls and plunging like a feathery plume it tickled the sandy bottom of the river, tickled so hard that up sprang Hiawatha with Minnehaha in his arms, two tawny brooms sprung from an opened closet.

# 10

I adjudge with rugged counseling I might cross that footbridge without jumping over the rail.

The unappetizing swell of the muddied water could appeal only to the truly desperate, the men with garters where stars were elsewhere strewn, or someone who got mixed up in his laces, or a shoe with a will of its own. Otherwise it was trudge trudge protected from the winter blast, but nudged along by cold, all the same. One remembered fireflies on the riverbanks and mosquitoes, the snow falling onto vanished wings, despair's equivalents of winter crossings.

Old Chinese men with shoulders bent under their thin kimonos passing over bamboo bridges. Mountain paths going ever upward into fog swirls.

# I I

Despising the heavy food that was going to give them all gout, as Arnholt always reminded Pedersen when they sat down at the long wooden tables in the University cafeteria expensively built to resemble a Swiss chalet (not a Chateau en Suède). There was such an anachronism lurking in the snakelike room that Pedersen frequently mistook the potatoes in his soup for boulders and searched beneath them for the hidden reptiles.

The Art Classes above the basement cafeteria clumped about and dragged things across the floor. "Picasso's heavy easel," murmured Arnholt. "With Las Meninas on it," shouted Pedersen.

## PRAIRIE HOUSES

Unreasonable lenses refract the
sensitive rabbit holes, mole dwellings and snake
climes where twist burrow and sneeze
a native species

into houses

corresponding to hemispheric requests
of flatness

euphemistically, sentimentally
termed prairie.

On the earth exerting a wilful pressure

something like a stethoscope against the breast

only permanent.

Selective engineering architectural submissiveness
and rendering of necessity in regard to height,
eschewment of climate exposure, elemental
       understandings,
constructive adjustments to vale and storm

historical reconstruction of early earthworks

and admiration

for later even oriental modelling

for a glimpse of baronial burdening
we see it in the rafters and the staircase heaviness
a surprise yet acting as ballast surely

the heavens strike hard on prairies.

Regard its hard-mouthed houses with their
robust nipples the gossamer hair.

# 13

The problem proposed to the lemon tree. When will your green fruit turn yellow? When shall I understand Minneapolis?

If not grain by grain, at least loaf by loaf.

If not the river flow, at least its turn and tributary.

Still there are permissions to approach through that immigrant air.

# 14

"The refinement of what's special takes place between the meat and the bun. N'est-ce-pas?" Signor Reboneri who was paying a visit to Minneapolis (well recompensed) insisted on this point in his lecture.

He had been somewhat influenced locally by a visit to the "1½", a bar frequented by Viking heroes, and his correspondences to the mythology of so-called "cruder" peoples, or bluntly "sauvages", was somewhat tempered by his excursions to the saloon. In fact, when dealing with the late Romans he was hard put to call one of their conquerors "a barbarian". The myth of the blond was gently settling over his own toga. He liked what he saw. The beer joint. The athletes still of medium weight, in their Atilla hiatus, i.e. the hefty maidens and the food as junky as that served in a mead hall.

Those slides with pillars and capitols soon to fall, accommodating his lectures, trod under by these self-same mythic hosts, required apologies. Never had he lamented more the Roman Empire's Fall. Never in his own bed had he envied more those thighs so decadent, delicious and declining as now when confronting these tribes! These god-like men! These Vikings! These hairy arms, blond, not swarthy. And these limbs any Caesar should welcome, if only the brutal club were hid. As now it was.

Signor Reboneri lent his curvaceous smile to the peanut strewn floor and ordered another brew.

# 15

## AT THE GUTHRIE THEATER

The lengthy slow cooking of the Children's Opera "Lentils" caused some consternation among the paying members who constituted at least a tenth of the Theater's subsidy. The rest, naturally, came from a State grant which to everyone's surprise turned out to be as unlimited as the grain supply. Yet here one must give due respect to the administrative abilities of its director, a native son, who unlike transplants was not prone to the cultural shock suffered by administrators shifted from New York or Washington or an Ivy League campus to these local art enclaves from whence they viewed the unmistakable disaster areas of Minneapolis.

*Au contraire,* as the Countess would humbly say, Helm Wulfings and his assistants: Hnaef Hocings, Wald Woings, Wod Thurings, Seaferth Seggs, "Swede" Ogentheow, Shafthere Ymbers, Shaefa Longbeards, Hun Hetwards, Holen Wrosns, Ringweald Raider, are true Deors, heroes *vraiment.* "Their enthusiasm," she would add, "is catching". She used some other word than that, possibly, *"Ils prennent la couverture",* but she meant their swordsmanship served us all.

## 16

"Amaryllis, favorite daughter,
I miss those long ago hours we shared, our mutual whisperings and field and town delights. I pray soon you will answer my letter so that this separation may find its fixity in the space dividing us, or rather, may enrich the space that separates us."

*"Like cat's moans, draughts soughing under*
*wooden doors. Whistles on the river.*
*The plunge of a floe when the wild*
*garbage flew past,*

> *yellow hair frost pinned . . .*
> *embers with their brilliant grins . . .*

*The sickening passages from Longfellow*
*stinking up the night, carapaces,*
*nerve castles strewn with aches and crunches*
*where the roof bone began to sag and thin.*

    I am writing this to you Father to give a true description of what the winter has been like:

> *not without pleasures altogether,*
> *disguised toes, heavy boots on the floor,*
> *the erotics of root cellars . . ."*

## PERSIANS IN MINNEAPOLIS

They are lithe, slim, dark. They
travel up and down the elevators all
the way to the thirtieth floor like slim
geniis emerging from their bottles.

No one knows why they are in Minneapolis.

The spring leaves which are thin and small
like Persians are closer to them
than anything else in this vast
brokeness of upset structures.

These Persians have a continuity which they
have left somewhere else and
this makes for surprise and
puzzlement. Not only for the
Persians, but for us who stand so
tall and thick beside them in
the elevator admiring Persian
determination and finally not finding
it reasonable without rugs beneath its feet.

# 18

The sunroom in the house on the river bank with the heavy rolltop desk, the desk evoking Ford Madox Ford. He wrote: "We used before 1914 to have the simple old view . . .

> *Que toutes les joies et tous honneurs*
> *viennent d'armes et d'amour.*

But upon these lines one could scarcely now conduct a life . . ."

The desk in the Minnesota twilight that edged in through each window a light the color of the lemony moustache of Ford Madox Ford. From here "a simple old view."

In the galaxy of apprehensions present tonight restraining oneself from adding to what should remain simple . . . leaving Madox with its single 'd'.

# 19

## (SCOP — A POET) WIDSITH

Scoping along the Mississippi. I a Scop. Coasting the Myth-West, musing the margins, earth yearned river wracked, grieving and groping, I a Scop making my weird. I saw many fellows, lithesome liquor hoarders, drawers of the dream, also riven by the river, daughter of the Rood. All have heard of the musicians ravishing, the museum-walker's mirth morsels, the lake Scops inland, inward impressing the bairns words, his ribbon of runes. Gusts from the Guthrie's stage spoken ear oaths, alas of an afternoon the wind sprung word tokens, host hoardings, sharers of sheaths, the frames of finished fine arts like jovial jousts surmounting the silence where prairie plumes cuddle and clash.

# 20

JOHN GRAHAM riding in his coach to meet the Countess stopped at the mansion of Larisnov on Summit Avenue for a sudden glass of tea. The two men strolled in the garden that overlooked the city of St. Paul commenting on the various fixtures and incompletions, the domes, the central plazas and that avid air of chance hanging, as always, over a capitol.

It was in that garden the laws of Minimalism as opposed to Baroque were formed and the great Futuristic statements came about, climaxing in "less is Mores" which led to a general razing of the remnants of the late nineteenth century that in their generous furry way were suffocating the capitol.

"Remember deterioration is embarrassing," added John Graham, (Ivan Dabrosky) and jumped into his carriage to continue on to his rendez-vous with the Countess.

# 21

"This street reminds me of scarceness, even loss like searching for hen's teeth in the rain," murmured the Countess to herself as she picked her way slowly down Hennepin Avenue. "I feel frightfully sad somehow and truly lost. I wish I had a glass of sherry right now, only that would never do. I mean I couldn't drink it here on the corner. Look at that gutter. So muddy. The wind's from the Southeast which should mean . . . I never know what it means. The prairies confuse me so. Perhaps Liv will have a hot bath ready when I finally reach home. That and the new frock from New York with the twin reveres. I wonder how reveres shall look on top of mutton sleeves. There's venison for supper. And the St. Louis Dispatch with luck should have arrived." The Countess hesitated for a moment as the sidewalk drifted into dirt and her grey eyes filled with dust.

## 22

Seated at the mirror rolling up her hair, feeling the thin papers curling around her fingers, the air in contrast thick from the low glaucous clouds, the color of flour, her fingers twisting the papers into shapes like grain bins — cylindrical . . . exactly the shape . . . remembering those one passed driving out over the rutted roads. The same routes she often dreamed of as passages to better things. Such as a lime laden or elm heavy driveway poised within a privacy, a refinement, a collection of tested images with their fragrances not here in the grain struck air, the summits of flour rising like pillows over the landscape. And her imagination hastened to where all was still, aged, and quartered.

The curl papers were shredded, dropped onto the floor, parquet as she had wished, yet so disturbed by its removal here to Minneapolis, broken in spots and mended that the surface reflected a suffering which she shared and thus its beauty still in shine (like hers) did little to comfort her. She tore into the curl papers as she would attack a silo, knowing she had rendered them useless as the silo wrestled from its usefulness would in turn relinquish the fortune that yet sustained her.

# 23

She waited. Within her limited mathematics she comprehended space. She understood the Dutch room in the paintings. The face behind the mirror. The walker in the dark. The captive tree. Not difficult. It was only within the picture she could breathe. A simple woman sat there wearing a cap, holding a pot. Another woman peered from a hall. You could sense how close the house was next door. The Countess worshipped that confinement, the enclosure of the scoured space. The eye never wandered far. The little mirror to tell you who walked in the street.

From where she sat there was the lake and she looked out on it. The further shore was now ripening. After that the flats. After that the river.

Her skin was growing rough. The wind placed a skull upon her face. Her face where it fell sideways had begun to toughen. It might grow to accommodate this life.

# 24

"What you need is a sophisticated cat."

The Countess reread the letter. Then opening her escritoire she took pen in hand and answered:

"Contact nearest available feline breeding — kennel — was it kennel — was it shed? Whatever. The sooner the better." And she would watch over it. It mustn't run wild, think itself a dog and have problems so difficult and different . . . especially those aristocrats. "Preferable non-pedigree", she wrote.

## 25

The further exoticism of reading a British novel while visiting Duluth. The Countess usually "tucked one into her dressing case" when preparing for a visit to one of Theodoric's relations. The excitement of the Lake precipitated an unconscious association with former boating parties when she had been younger and, alas, inhabited a narrower world.

"Rather like reading of the River Niger while dining alone in New York," sympathized her cousin, Glanville.

# 26

When the scandal about Eofirth broke out the Countess vanished into her bedroom giving orders that no one should be admitted, especially Theodoric who would take it upon himself to bring her all the newspapers with the interviews, etc. One could hear, as if emerging from a shelf under old newspapers, the music, "Songs From The Auvergne" which the countess perversely kept listening to.

"Of course", she repeated as she paced the room, "Eofirth could not be guilty of any higgledypiggledy. He was always totally honest and with everyone with whom he had associated.

"Tax fraud! How absurd."

No one with his talents, a real artist, could ever be absolutely above board. Seduction, yes, and domination. But as for cheating! And money! He hid his money under those gilded coaches and in the rooms of those spidery summerhouses. Also in caves, she suspected, where the water might tease it a bit. He was capable of depositing sums with the captain who took the boat back and forth to Eofirth's island.

Eofirth. She remembered his first chess game. His first circus. His tears when age began to beckon those close to him. His first marriage and the scenes from his last one.

His was the only icey hand with any warmth concealed in it. It was he who had called her "my light in winter". Who had led her in a northern country to the first wild strawberry.

She hid under the quilt refusing to hear his impassioned, "I'll immigrate! I'll immigrate!" savaging the room.

Don't Eofirth, she cried, abandon me to these nerveless plains. This forgetful river. You who have made Christ swing from a tree. Who have commanded dwarfs. Never forget the loneliness of Strindberg in Paris. And never, like that other well-known exile, film the politics of loss.

# 27

Reality's tramline intruded.

"Köttbullar med gräddsky!" shouted Liv from the first landing.

The Countess arose. Dabbed her temples with Cologne 711 and seizing a small ripe cherry cane on which to rest the remnants of her grief, descended. The soothing aroma of cream, meat, and onion overpowered her remorse.

If only Eofirth were here to share the cranberry jelly and pickled cucumber.

# 28

"Everything I've told you is true," said Lars.

"But I want to see our son." When the Countess said 'son' one almost heard a faint Baltic accent. Possibly. Language intensifies.

"I would never cheat you in the photographs. My lens are accurate. I only use the fog swirls when necessary. Lately I'm ashamed of those early pictures of him I sent you. They were too romantic. I even shot them in rooms with red walls. I've learned much. I can call his face and he responds. See how real, how much truth there is in this photograph of our son?"

"I wanted something more than the definition of a shoulder."

"I gave you his clarity."

"Yet in these pictures he is so quiet. I want to see him move."

"A photograph can only indicate. If this stillness broke, the picture would blur."

"I would love that blur."

"I cannot go against my craft."

"Then I can only guess how his head turns when it escapes his shoulder?"

"Yes. My camera gives you that permission."

## 29

Driving away from the logging camp, despite the severity, the opinions, the formalism which surrounded Lars, the Countess felt again that something heavier than air escaping her lungs. Later lying quietly on the pine needles while he arranged his camera, admiring as always, his adroitness, the rapidity with which his preparations took place as just before the shutter fell his lens sheltered her face.

## 30

Outside through the window she believed she could see the prophet Elijah, his sunken face pressed against the glass, peering past the angular whisper of the blue flower petals.

## 31

It is here those lives with their difficult parts, their sidelines of disaster. My lot, even if I cannot reach them, yet I sympathize. My isolation is cushioned. From the prairie, the wind teasing the dogs. Someday within my fingers this skein will untangle. Then the region becomes a fairy tale with steeples and castles. Now there are sod huts. My broken slipper leaves few splinters on this path. Perhaps the mocassins . . .

## 32

There was a poem with
A Moon in it travelling across the bridge in one
Of those fragile trains carrying very small loads
Like moons that one could never locate anywhere else.
The Mississippi was bright under the bridge like a
Sun, because the poem called itself the Sun also;
Two boxcars on the bridge crossing the river.

# 33

Countess:

Correspondences Peking-Tokyo their comparisons and differences in her character

or the Shanghai-Peking axis

consult oriental arbiter

And still she said,
walking toward Crocus Hill Market,
one desires to live. I wish there
were wishes and not lists.
I wish vegetables were grown
by heart and artichokes would heal,
I wish this rhythm
of my approaching the butcher
were more than a knuckle
attaching itself to me
perhaps a crocus, a
root of limited possibilities,
yet promising a livelihood.

## CROCUS HILL

I had dreamed the night before I awakened that morning I would be on Crocus Hill. First we lost our way then entered the Freeway then left that for Summit Hill. Whereupon the towers of St. Paul stared up at us. It was interesting architecturally; geographically speaking, where was Crocus Hill? I was thinking about tomatoes, Apollinaire water, kidneys, sweetbreads, truffles, limes, Crocus Hill the finest grocery store in St. Paul. Finally after crossing, recrossing, submerging, indigent technical encounters of bumps — discovered. On the long polished counter expressive items breathed expressively and even husks luxuriated, cross pollinations from Eastern sources experimenting in historical fineries. From the counter the telephone rang.

 Madam! Immediately!
Choice! Prime! Tender! Aged! Fresh!

 Madam!

The Countess was ordering.

# 36

Heliogobalus, Heliograph, Heliology, Helium, Heliotrope, Haiti . . .

The Countess scanned the map for Carribean Kingdoms. Borrowing a piece of burlap she had been intrigued by its aroma of palms and her day began to be replaced by exotic blossoms and sea airs. That Chantey her uncle had taught her began to echo and she tried a limited sailor's hornpipe on the rug Theodoric had purchased in Constantinople.

She supposed after swabbing down the deck one might dance a hornpipe. If one were a Scottish sailor becalmed on the morning Sargossa Sea.

Idly, because she was often idle, she traced with her nail the mountain path up from the port, sheltering under one of those tropical trees as the rain blew up and birds fled past, their brilliancy lighting her face. Her skin's sallow inwardness turned outwards as unexpectedly the sun struck.

A toning like a tuning began to strum her nerves. Like an excellent massage this journey she was making. A purr sounded throughout the motor system. Sun piercingly yellow. Her face changed color and once more a tiny parade crossed her temples.

## 37

## ACTIVITIES

Grain Belt Beer, He Who Gets Slapped, Vikings vs Dolphins, ice skating, fishing, Japanese food, meat, square dancing, collage, Rimbaud, New York Painting, Showboats, Baskin-Robbins ice cream, La Strada, Basement Studios, renting a house, visiting lecturers, tourist flights to Scandinavia, Crystal Court lunches, Dayton's cotton undies, leather shops, Indian crafts, jazz, blizzards, mosquitoes, Betty Crocker recipes, Lake Superior Poetry, silos, covered bridges, Artichoke Hall, brawls, aftermaths, forecasts, illegal turns, incontinent highways, building, building, building, razing, razing, razing, Milwaukee complexes, abandonment, lost frontiers, height, girth, pride, prejudice, toughness, agoraphobia, agoraphilia, alewifehood, navigations, symphonies, tornadoes, sauna construction . . .

nostalgia for the days when one searched for furniture those pre-Saarinen days. For some the pre-Aalto decade.

## 38

The hints of ruggedness, such as the
window's slipshod, the twist where
the sash should have fallen true. Dark
objects falling. They were permitted to fall
because their characters at first were not
dark, merely fringes, one guessed. Later
when the axes appeared like meanings, we
understood but it was too late. "I have
explained this to you before, Countess, and
there were those wrenches at the end, whenever
Ingmar came to the conclusion of his story."
"Only a warning," he said, rising from where
he was sitting. "I cherish you."
She nodded, as was her custom. "I only bring
warnings like lesions, so you may know the true
nature of this weather." He kissed her.
And that, also, was his custom.

## JUNE

dust dust dust dust dust dust
only small rain small rain small
thin thin rain starved rain rin

# 40

She waited on the terrace for him to arrive, a small nut in its shell on the terrace. The little wife in a tale sitting in her rocker in her shell house. She read stories and told them back again to herself, rehearsing, memorizing what she was doing while she waited. The sun ripened, fell. The water receptive reflected the illusions the sky was trying out; those illusions flitted away. The sky became exhausted with its innumerable positions, its plans. And she, she curled up in her shell and went to sleep, because somewhere else in the Village he had made other arrangements.

Originally the Walker Art Museum was formed from the nucleus of the Walker Chinese Collection. Even now there is a minor space relegated to the once sacred and exotic collection. There are disturbing moments when one comes upon cities carved in jade, oarsmen, mountaineers, flocks of bird and cattle, tribes far from the palatial coastal cities. There is activity and there is repose and especially magical the jade mountain where:

> "In the beginning of the late spring, a gathering was held at Lan T'ing for the purpose of repairing the graves. All the celebrities came. At this place there were steep mountains and magnificent mountain ranges, heavy frosts and graceful bamboo plants. There was also a clear rapid running brook. One cup of wine and one poem were enough to bring out the hidden emotions."
> CHING DYNASTY
> 1784 A.D.
> (The Emperor Ch'ien Lung)

From here it is only necessary to mount the staircase thus transcending one hundred and ninety two years to the sculpture roof garden where Tony Smith has bestowed his *Amaryllis*.

## AMARYLLIS

The orange metal plant spread its tendrils aloof over the museum's roof. With all its fragrant captivity asserting the immigrant rites of sculpture.

Restrained by metal from whispering, from complaint, even from homesickness, Amaryllis with its antique name, its distant origins, held a regal stance.

Between its position and the blockades of the city, between it and the nearest reliquary there would remain no communion. Amaryllis would never yield its superior stance. Its moods, glances, were those of an observer less restless as time passed, yet one who possessed the claim to restrict its grace.

There could be detected something of the borrower here, rather than the lender, an attitude the Museum's curator recognized would never change. He questioned the effect of those regal metal blooms upon the visitors. He worried if the city were aware of the undisturbed and selfish enchantment Amaryllis cast. A piece of art that through a collector's whim had come to dwell in Minneapolis.

*This book was printed on 60 lb. Glatfelter (an acid-free paper) and smyth-sewn into paper covers by Thomson-Shore in Dexter, MI. It is offset from the original letterpress edition set in 11 pt. Caledonia and designed by Rosmarie Waldrop. The cover design by Keith Waldrop uses Robert Koehler's painting* Rainy Evening on Hennepin Avenue *by courtesy of the Minneapolis Institute of Arts.*